TIBERIAS
AND THE SEA OF GALILEE

BONECHI & STEIMATZKY

CONTENTS

© Copyright 1993 by CASA EDITRICE BONECHI
Via Cairoli, 18b 50131 Firenze - Italia
Tel. 55/576841 - Telex 571323 CEB - Fax 55/5000766

Printed in Italy by
Centro Stampa Editoriale Bonechi

Photographs from the archives of Casa Editrice Bonechi
taken by *Paolo Giambone.*

Photo on page 23 below: kindly provided by the *Kibbutz Ginnosar.*

Text by: *Giuliano Valdes, Editing Studio - Pisa*

Translation by: *Julia Weiss*

ISBN 88-8029-067-3

INTRODUCTION

The emerald green waters of the Sea of Galilee break up the unusual and fascinating landscape of the Jordan River Valley in the northeastern part of Israel that extends like a wedge between Lebanon on the west and Syria to the east. It is also known as the Sea of Tiberias or Lake of Gennesaret; in Hebrew it is called Yam Kinneret and in Arabic, Buhayrat Tabariya. The name Sea of Tiberias derives from the city on its western shore that was founded by Herod Antipas and named for the ruling emperor Tiberius. The Hebrew name, Kinneret, may come from the language's word for "harp", Kinnor, and in fact the lake is shaped like an ancient harp.

This small inland sea, set like an emerald amongst the hills of the Galilee to the west, and the Golan Heights to the east, is dominated to the north by Mount Hermon which, from its 2814 meters overlooks much of the Middle East. Its snow-capped peaks perpetuate the memory of ancient Phoenician cults and episodes from the Old Testament. The Sea of Galilee originated towards the end of the Tertiary Period following a catastrophe which created the great depression of the Jordan, and is part of the Great Eastern Rift. The sea is 21 kilometers long, 12 kilometers across at its widest point and has a total surface area of 166 square kilometers. It is situated in a depression, 212 meters below sea level and its maximum depth is 48 meters. According to some sources it reaches to a depth of 250 meters in the middle. It is bordered by basalt deposits (the Golan Heights are partly vulcanic in origin) while the hills of the Galilee, though morphologically varied, do share a common calcareous matrix. The sea is fed primarily by the Jordan River which is the only river flowing into its northern portion. Plains of alluvial origin extend north and south; the fertile regions surrounding the lake are dotted by rural settlements. This lake is a vital water reserve for the entire country. A large duct, conveys water as far as the Negev Desert in the southernmost part of Israel. The temperature ranges from average of 7.4°C in January to 31°C in July. Winter rainfall is around 450 mm. Even the vegetation has its distinguishing features for such a limited area. While olive and banana trees flourish near the shores, the hills are covered by lush Mediterranean plants. Going north towards Mount Hermon the vegetation becomes distinctly Alpine.

Due to the natural beauty of the landscape and mild climate near the lake, the area had been settled from earliest antiquity. In more general terms, like the rest of the Holy Land of which the sea is a significant part, we can say that this land has always been a meeting point for different peoples; for millenia it has been a link between customs and trade coming from Europe, Asia and Africa. Then, this vital setting has a religious aspect so that this corner of the Middle East is an essential crossroads for the great monotheistic religions: Christianity, Judaism and Islam that share a common root and extraordinary points of convergence.

The Sea of Galilee and its immediate surroundings were the site of some of the major episodes in the story of Jesus: whose life, teachings, miracles and final sacrifice on the Cross all took place here in the Holy Land. This land is the territory of the Old Testament and the Gospel. It is also the historical legacy and act of faith of an entire nation; it is the theater of Mohammed's mystical ascent to heaven. For Christians the Galilee was the setting for some of the most significant events recounted in the Gospels. As in Mark (IV, 35-41): "...And the same day, when the even was come, he saith unto them, Let us pass over unto the other side.

And when they had sent away the multitude, they took him even as he was in the ship. And there were also with him other little ships.

And there arose a great storm of wind, and the waves beat into the ship so that it was now full.

And he was in the hinder part of the ship, asleep on a pillow: and they awake him, and say unto him, Master, carest thou not that we perish?

And he arose, and rebuked the wind, and said unto the sea, Peace, be still. And the wind ceased, and there was a great calm.

And he said unto them, Why are ye so fearful. how is it that ye have no faith?

And they feared exceedingly, and said one to another, What manner of man is this, that even the wind and the sea obey him?..."

(Mark VI, 47-50):"...And when even was come, the ship was in the midst of the sea, and he alone on the land.

And he saw them toiling in rowing; for the wind was contrary unto them: and about the fourth watch of the night he cometh unto them, walking upon the sea, and would have passed by them.

But when they saw him walking upon the sea, they supposed it had been a spirit, and cried out:

For they all saw him, and were troubled. And immediately he talked with them, and saith unto them, Be of good cheer: it is I; be not afraid..."; and Luke (V, 1-7) "...as the people pressed upon him to hear the word of God, he stood by the Lake of Gennesaret,

And saw two ships standing by the lake: but the fishermen were gone out of them, and were washing their nets.

And he entered into one of the ships, which was Simon's, and prayed him that he would thrust out a little from the land. And he sat down, and taught the people out of the ship.

Now when he had left speaking, he said unto Simon, Launch out into the deep, and let down your nets for a draught.

And Simon answered said unto him, Master, we have toiled all the night, and have taken nothing: nevertheless at thy word I will let down the net.

And when they had this done, they inclosed a great multitude of fishes: and their net brake.

And they beckoned unto their partners, which were in the other ship, they they should come and help them. And they came, and filled both the ships, so that they began to sink..."; and Matthew (IV, 18-22): "...And Jesus, walking by the sea of Galilee, saw two brethren, Simon called Peter, and Andrew his brother, casting a net into the sea: for they were fishers.

And he saith unto them, Follow me, and I will make you fishers of men.

And they straightway left their nets, and followed him.

And going on from thence, he saw other two brethren, James the son of Zebedee, and John his brother, in a ship with Zebedee their father, mending their nets; and he called them.

And they immediately left the ship and their father, and followed him...."

Today, the Sea of Galilee, with its many fish, is a popular vacation place and its thermal springs make it a fine health resort as well.

Tiberias and its lake seen from En Gev.

A panorama of Tiberias and the Sea of Galilee.

TIBERIAS

The ancient capital of the Lower Galilee is essentially a modern town situated on the bare slopes of the western shore of the lake. It enjoys a fine reputation as tourist and health resort, which actually extends back to antiquity.

Tiberias was founded in the early part of the first century A.D., and exactly in the year 20, when Herod Antipas, son of Herod the Great decided to build a city on the site of an ancient fortified citadel in an area already known for its hot springs. Initially, the discovery of a large area used a burial ground stopped the more orthodox Jews who considered those places as unclean from settling there. The name *Tiberias* by which it has been called since then, proves that it was selected to honor the reign-

ing Roman emperor. The first settlement, built on the Hellenistic model, developed and grew, it coined its own money and made its own laws. Conquered by the Romans shortly before the fall of Jerusalem which took place in 70 AD, the city received great impetus for growth and cultural development. Many Jews moved there as did several important religious academies that made major contributions to the *Mishna* and the *Talmud*, the authoritative compilation of law, lore and commentary. For a certain time, the Sanhedrin assembled there and the population grew to over 40,000. Notwithstanding Jesus' repeated appearances in this part of the Galilee, Tiberias only receives marginal mention in the Gospels. The place which, in the meantime had be-

The ancient ruins of Tiberias blend harmoniously with the modern city, its avenues and buildings. Here we can see the Citadel reflected in the Sea of Galilee and some ruins of the ancient walls.

A modern Auditorium stands near the archeological gardens.

come one of the four holy cities of Judaism, acquired a certain importance in the spreading of Christian doctrine around the VI century, the late period of Byzantine rule.

In the early VII century Tiberias came under Arab control, to be reconquered by the Christians during the XII century Crusades, and it was the Crusaders who governed along the lines laid out under the Arab dominion. After the battle of Hattin (1187) when Saladin brought about the end of crusader power, Tiberias began its gradual decline. It was reduced to a heap of rubble and would remain abandoned for a long time. In the second half of the XVI

Two views of modern downtown Tiberias where tourists and vacationers can meet, shop and relax in the cafés.

An impressive view of the Grand Mosque.

Two details of the marina: here too, modern and ancient come together in pleasing contrast enlivened by the warm, solar colors of summer lights in this part of the Galilee.

Above: the "Galilee Experience", a new lakeside attraction, offers a full panorama of Tiberias history. Below: a ferry boat carries passengers across the Sea of Galilee.

The Tomb of Rabbi Akiba and two pictures of the Tomb of "Rambam" or Moses Maimonides. Many religious and philosophical schools flourished at Tiberias: and some of the greatest sages taught there.

century the Turkish sultan Sulayman the Magnificent tried to revive the city by granting it to his advisor the Portugese Don José, Duke of Naxos and his mother-in-law Doña Gracia Mendes. Their attempts to promote silkworm cultivation and textile "manufacturing" in the area failed. The economic recovery of Tiberias and its rebirth only occurred in the XVIII century when it was governed by the Bedouin chieftain, Daher el-Amar. After the War of Independence in 1948 which returned the city to the Jewish State, Tiberias grew into one of the most populated cities in the district and one of the most attractive tourist resorts because of the fine areas around the lake.

A succession of natural disasters (earthquakes) and intermittent wars through the centuries changed the appearance of the place so that today only few traces of its illustrious past can be seen. However, what does remain fits into the charming framework of the "coastal" city which is characterized by much greenery, and avenues flanked by palm trees. The big hotels, modern housing and business centers harmonize well with the older and markedly eastern style buildings. The guest facilities, which range from grand hotels to campsites, recreational and amusement areas meet the needs of both the most elegant clientele as well as those of mass tourism. The fish-filled waters of the Sea of Galilee (fishing is still a major source of income) are also well suited to the most popular water sports (swimming, waterskiing and motorboat racing).

The thermal springs at Tiberias have been known for over two thousand years. According to an ancient legend the springs were created by King

A colorful evening view of the marina, with the city's lights reflected in the lake.

Modern hotels, surrounded by palm trees flank the road to Hammat.

A hotel's gardens at the Hammat spa complex.

Solomon who ordered the demons to heat the waters of the springs. Today the spa season runs from October to May, thanks to the mild microclimate along the shores of the Galilee and the generally pleasant weather in the Jordan Valley. The waters, of vulcanic origin, are slightly radioactive, mineral-containing and saline and reach a temperature of about 60°C. The **new spa complex** provides all comforts and facilities for thermal cures. Physiotherapy and rehabilitation work are done in modern structures which include indoor and outdoor thermal pools.

Ruins of an ancient **tower**, sections of **wall** and other bits of antiquity made of dark basalt stone bear witness to the crusader settlement which was actually much smaller than the Tiberias of Herod's day.

The **citadel**, which gives a picturesque touch to the shoreline, enlivened by reflections of the ancient walls and a round tower between palm trees and plants, dates from the crusades even if the existing structure was rebuilt around the middle of the XVIII century by the Bedouin sheik Daher el Amar. The fortress withstood Ottoman attacks and allowed the shiek to extend his power to those territories which today comprise the northern part of Israel. Upon the death of the shiek, assassinated by an Ottoman plot (1775), the citadel was rebuilt by the Turks who used it for a prison. Today it is used for cultural (exhibitions, fairs, etc.) and recreational purposes.

Other points of interest include the **Grand Mosque**. It is made of basalt stone and is crowned by a hemispheric dome and a slim minaret; the **Tomb of Rabbi Akiba,** martyred by the Romans in 135 A.D.; and the **Tomb of Rambam** or Moses Maimonides the great Medieval Jewish philospher, jurist and physician (XII-XIII centuries) who was born in Cordoba (Spain) under Moslem domination and wanted to be buried in the holy city of Tiberias.

The interesting ruins of the Great Synagogue at Hammat fit into a picturesque landscape.

A detail of the mosaic floor depicting the Zodiac.

HAMMAT

South of Tiberias, along the road that flanks the western shore of the Sea of Galilee, and near an area dedicated to a National Park, rises the town of Hammat. It was known to the Romans for the beneficial properties of its thermal waters. Its name, in fact, comes from the Hebrew "ham" for "hot", and probably referred to the thermal waters. It seems that the first settlements in the area date from Biblical times. During the early sixties when work was being done to harness the thermal springs, some striking archeological finds were brought to light.

It is interesting to note that the town, which is just a few kilometers from Tiberias, and its history date farther back than that of the capital city. Here it is

possible to see traces of the ancient city founded by Herod Antipas and the ruins of the **Roman Baths**, located near a small museum dedicated to the baths. The most interesting place for visitors and the archeologically most significant (along with the remains of other, smaller synagogues, one of which dates from the III century A.D.) is the remains of the **Great Synagogue**. This is one of the finest examples of Greco-Byzantine art in the Holy Land. The splendid floor mosaics in this building that can be dated around the IV century A.D. are of great artistic value in addition to being beautiful. One of these, still *in situ*, is right near an apsidal structure in an impressive setting with a magnificent view of the sea and its surrounding hills. Near the entrance

we can see Greek and Aramaic inscriptions thanking those whose generosity made it possible to build the synagogue. The center part of the mosaic shows the *Wheel of the Zodiac* with the *Four Seasons* in the corners. At the top we can see objects related to *Jewish rituals and religious practices*. In the same area we can also see two large prayer rooms, one datable around the VI-VII century and the other from about one hundred years later.

Not far from the baths are some buildings of clearly Islamic style. Inside, in dark basalt stone, topped by a colored, hemispheric dome is the **Tomb of Rabbi Meir Baal ha-Nes,** who lived in the II century D.C. and was known as "The Miracle Worker". This group of buildings also includes two Talmud schools.

Two views of the archeological digs at Hammat showing the remains of the Great Synagogue.

The Tomb of Rabbi Meir Baal ha-Nes seen from the outside, and a detail of the interior.

HORNS OF HATTIN

These mountains with their rocky outlines dominate the horizon over the Sea of Galilee, rising to the west of Tiberias. Their origins are definitely volcanic, but their importance – aside from mere orientation and color in the lovely natural setting that surrounds the Sea – is related to a specific historical event.

It was here that on 5 July 1187 the Crusaders were soundly defeated by Saladin's armies. The unhappy conclusion of this battle marked the end of the first Crusader kingdom in the Holy Land.

Nearby, at Nebi Shueib, the Druze community worships the tomb of Jethro, father-in-law of Moses.

The ancient synagogue at Hammat: detail of the interior.

Tiberias: an impressive view of the Sea of Galilee.

The Horns of Hattin.

Looking towards the Sea of Galilee, the architecture is reminiscent of Orthodox churches.

A detail of the Yigal Allon Center where the boat from Jesus' era is displayed.

The boat dating from Jesus' era is on display at the Yigal Allon Center.

The gardens of Ginnosar and the Tomb of Yigal Allon.

The lakeshore at Ginnosar.

GINNOSAR

North of Tiberias there is a broad, flat area characterized by an extraordinary abundance of crops and extremely fertile soil: this is the Valley of Ginnosar. The area had already been extensively described by the Jewish Roman historian, Josephus Flavius (I century A.D.) in his book *The Jewish Wars,* as a magnificent place where "…. there is not a plant that does not flourish there, and the inhabitants grow everything: the air is so temperate that it suits the most diverse species." In fact, even today, this generous land produces olives, lemons and bananas as well as typically tropical fruits such as mangoes, pecans and avocado pears.

Tabgha, the Church of the Miracle of the Loaves and the Fishes.

A detail of the cloister overlooking the Church of the Miracle of the Loaves and the Fishes.

An ancient olive press at Tabgha.

In the vineyards grapes are ripe by the end of May and many out-of-season fruits flourish thanks to the mild lakeside climate.

Kibbutz Ginnosar is located near the shore in a wonderful natural setting. It's a green and fertile oasis which, since its founding in 1937, has become a true earthly paradise. Surrounded by crops, gardens and flowering plants stands the **Nof Ginnosar Guest House.** This fully-equipped establishment is ideal for rests and holidays, and is a perfect starting point for excursions to nearby places of interest. The **tomb of Yigal Allon,** a simple rock with Hebrew inscriptions, is located in the park.

The most interesting item for visitors in this area, however, is related to a sensational archeological discovery made in 1986 on the shores of the Sea of Galilee between the Kibbutz Ginnosar and Migdal. An extended drought revealed a **boat** from 2,000 years ago, which was excellently preserved by the clayey soil. After some preliminary work it was put on display in a specially equipped pool at the *Yigal Allon Center.* Experts have dated it between the I century BC and the I century AD. And so, even if this is not "Jesus' boat" as many newspapers hastened to report, it certainly can shed light on a fascinating chapter in the area's history.

TABGHA

"And when it was evening, his disciples came to him, saying, This is a desert place, and the time is now past; send the multitude away, that they may go into the villages, and buy themselves victuals. But Jesus said unto them, They need not depart; give ye them to eat. And they said unto him, we have here but five loaves, and two fishes. He said, Bring them hither to me. And he commanded the multitude to sit down on the grass, and took the five loaves, and the two fishes, and looking up to heaven, he blessed, and brake, and gave the loaves to his disciples, and the disciples to the multitude. And they did all eat, and were filled: and they took up of the fragments that remained twelwe baskets full. And they that had eaten were about five thousand men, beside women and children" (Matthew, XIV 15-21).

The place where this occurred, situated near the Sea of Galilee on the slopes of the Mount of Beatitudes, is known locally also as *Tabgha.* This name is the Arab version of a Greek word whose meaning seems from its sound to be "seven fountains"

(*Heptapegon*). There are, in fact, some sulphurous springs in the area, once much prized and frequented because they cured skin diseases. According to tradition, it was by bathing in one of these springs that Job was cured of leprosy. Recently the waters have been found to be quite radioactive, so that their therapeutic use is not advised.

But the aspect of Tabgha which principally arouses the interest of visitors is the existence of two churches commemorating two well-known episodes in the life of Jesus, the multiplication of the loaves and fishes and the third appearance to his disciples after the Resurrection.

CHURCH OF THE MIRACLE OF THE LOAVES AND THE FISHES - It is a modern building standing on the site of a fourth century Byzantine church, built where Jesus was sitting while he performed one of his best known miracles. The ancient church, already damaged by earth-

These pictures show the interior of the Church of the Miracle of the Loaves and the Fishes at Tabgha. Note the overview of the church, the detail of the presbytery with the main altar, and the mosaic floor; two details of the splendid floor mosaics in this house of worship.

quakes in the sixth century, was completely destroyed a century later. All trace and even memory of it was lost, until the XIX century when Benedictine monks uncovered its interesting ruins. The interior of the basilica follows the classical pattern for this type of building: nave and aisles, transept, apse and narthex. What makes this church one of the sights most frequently visited by tourists is the mosaic decoration. Considered one of the finest examples of this in the Holy Land, the mosaics of the Church of the Miracle of the Loaves and the Fishes stand out for their vibrant colors and for the fine execution of decorative motifs, such as the animals and plants typical of the surroundings of the lake. But the most praised and best known mosaic is certainly the one which symbolically depicts the miracle after which the church is named: it shows a *basket full of loaves between two fishes*. Below the high altar is a stone marking the place where Christ put down the two fishes and five loaves.

Two impressive views of the Church of the Primacy of St. Peter at Tabgha, reflected in the blue waters of the Sea of Galilee, and a detail of the Mensa Christi.

CHURCH OF THE PRIMACY OF ST. PETER -

This Christian temple rises near the shore of the lake with an evocative and picturesque landscape as its setting. The church was built by the Franciscans, in the nineteen forties, in dark blocks of basalt rock. From very ancient times there has been a rock there (it may now be seen inside the church) which was known by the Latin name of *Mensa Christi*. It is said that on that rock Jesus conferred on Peter the responsibility of being the future head of the Church. The Gospel tells how Christ appeared to his disciples for the third time after the Resurrection and how the primacy of Peter was then affirmed. "After these things Jesus shewed himself again to the disciples at the Sea of Galilee; ...He saith unto him the third time, Simon, son of Jonas, lovest thou me? Peter was grieved because he said unto him, the tird time, Lovest thou me? And he said unto him Lord, thou knowest all things; thou knowest that I love thee. Jesus saith unto him, Feed my sheep" (John, XXI 1 and 17).

Capernaum: views of the ancient ruins of a third- or fourth-century Synagogue.

CAPERNAUM

"And they went into Capernaum; and straight-way on the sabbath day he entered into the synagogue, and taught" (Mark, I 21). "And thou, Capernaum, which art exalted unto heaven, shalt be brought down to hell: for if the mighty works, which have been done in thee, had been done in Sodom, it would have remained until this day. But I say unto you, That it shall be more tolerable for the land of Sodom in the day of judgement than for thee" (Matthew, XI 23-24).

The archeological site of Capernaum is all that is left of a city once extremely prosperous and impor-tant, especially in the period when Jesus was preaching. The Hebrew name of *Kefar Nahum* can be heard again today, as the name of some very con-siderable ruins standing where the Jordan runs into the Sea of Galilee. An important road once passed (and still passes) there, over which the caravans

made their way to Syria. Capernaum is mentioned many times in the Gospels. As well as the verses quoted above, there are accounts of several miracles performed by Jesus in that city, such as the resurrection of the daughter of the alderman of the synagogue: "And he took the damsel by the hand, and said unto her, Talitha cumi; which is, being interpreted, Damsel, I say unto thee, arise" (Mark, V 41); the healing of the centurion's servant (Luke, VII 1-10), and the chasing out of an unclean spirit from a man in the synagogue (Mark, I 23-26). In spite of the many miracles performed at Capernaum, as well as in other cities, the inhabitants were not converted, which provoked the bitter reproof of Christ, and especially the prophecy of evil directed at Capernaum itself.

The interesting remains of an ancient *Synagogue*, dating from the third or fourth century, are the most conspicuous landmark in the city, once splendid but fallen into decay and ruin with irreversible damage done by earthquakes and war. It is almost possible to believe, on rereading the verses from Matthew,

HAND-MILLS

VIA MARIS
MILESTONE

Capernaum: the ruins of an ancient Byzantine church, supposed to have been once the House of Simon Peter, and other architectual remains.

Capernaum: among the ruins it is possible to distinguish the remains of an ancient mill, a Roman milestone, frangments of a mosaic and a broken pillar with a Corinthian capital.

that Jesus' prophecy has been exactly fulfilled. The synagogue, where we can admire the remains of the limestone walls, the pillars with their fine Corinthian capitals, and the decorated fragments of beams, has no connection with the synagogue where Christ taught, nor the one built by the centurion whose servant was miraculously healed. It is believed that this one was built in the late imperial age, under the Emperor Julian, and is one of a series of similar religious buildings that arose in the upper part of Galilee with the financial support of the imperial authorities. This supposition appears to be confirmed by the presence of decorative elements, such as griffons, eagles, lions, dates, acanthus, seashells and others, which are usually prohibited Jewish places of worship.

Not far from the synagogue are the remains of an ancient building - in all probability a Byzantine church - which tradition holds to be the *House of Simon Peter.*

MOUNT OF BEATITUDES

This so called "mount" is a hill situated above the Sea of Galilee, in a remarkably fine landscape. It is named after the Sermon on the Mount, during which Jesus proclaimed the Beatitudes to the crowd that had gathered to listen to him (Matthew, V 3-11).

The Church of the Beatitudes at the top of the hill was built in 1937 by the architect Antonio Barluzzi. This remarkable building is octagonal in structure. On the outside there is a colonnaded portico which runs right round the building. A bell gable stands in front of the dome, which is supported by an octagonal tambour. Inside, the eight windows each bear the text of the beginning of one of the Beatitudes pronounced by Jesus during the Sermon on the Mount.

Mount of Beatitudes: view of the hill with the church of the same name and a glimpse of the Sea of Galilee from the church portico.

Church of Beatitudes: from top to bottom and left to right: front view of the church; the high altar; the inside of the cupola.

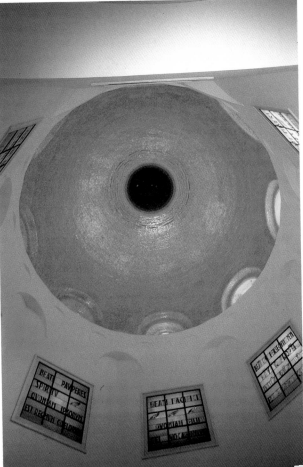

Some of the excavations at Chorazin, with the ruins of the ritual baths and ancient dark basalt stone buildings.

CHORAZIN

The interesting archeological area of Chorazin is just a short distance from the northern shore of the Sea of Galilee, in the lower part of the hills between the Nahal Amud and Jordan rivers, creating the northern border of the basin. The ancient city of Chorazin, which was razed to the ground by an earthquake in the III century A.D. along with nearby Bethsaida, dared to defy Christ by refusing to follow his teachings. These episodes are clearly retold in the Gospels according to Luke and Matthew, with the harsh words Jesus had for the two rebellious cities: "...Then began he to upbraid the cities wherein most of his mighty works were done, because they repented not:
Woe unto thee, Chorazin! woe unto thee, Bethsaida! for if the mighty works, which were done in you had been done in Tyre and Sidon, they would have repented long ago in sackcloth and ashes.
But I say unto you, It shall be more tolerable for Tyre and Sidon at the day of judgement than for you..." (Matthew, XI, 20-22).
The earliest archeological excavations at the site of the ancient city of Chorazin were conducted in 1905. The finds were of great architectural interest: some portals, friezes, capitals and cornices in elaborately carved stone were brought to light. Further excavations were done in the mid-twenties and in 1968 when a settlement, adjacent to the synagogue was uncovered.
The **synagogue**, or rather, what remains of it is definitely of greatest interest for vistors. The vestiges of the building that date from somewhere between the

The ancient synagogue at Chorazin and some details; the steps and some of the columns supporting part of the trabeation and frieze are recognizable; this building too was made of dark basalt.

III and IV centuries A.D. fit perfectly into the already impressive natural environment. Most of the dark basalt ruins are scattered on the ground, while a few of the columns that supported parts of the trabeation and frieze are still standing. The main decorative motifs were on the southern wall, facing Jerusalem. The assumptions put forward by archeologists and architects would tell us that the synagogue was at least two stories high and in any event, its central portion was higher than the rest of the building It seems certain that the builders of the Chorazin synagogue were inspired by the model at nearby Capernaum. Other buildings have been found north of the synagogue, and we know for certain that some comprised the *mikvah*, that is, the **ritual baths.** The most unusual feature of the buildings at Chorazin is that the "city's roofs formed a wall".

The Jordan Park and two views of En Gev with its dock and gardens overlooking the Sea of Galilee.

THE JORDAN PARK

Known locally as *Park Hayarden*, this park is located above the Sea of Galilee where Israel's major river flows into the sea. The park's setting itself is quite beautiful, near the Bethsaida Valley. To the northwest the horizon is dominated by the mountains that separate the Galilee from Lebanon while the Golan Heights soar on the east. Some of the points of interest include a suspension bridge, the ruins of a crusader fortress and a windmill. The park's attractions fit neatly into a naturalistic context characterized by papyrus and reeds, cactus, flowers and willow trees. Recreational facilities such as picnic areas and some small waterfalls that delight the younger visitors complete the panorama of a place where contact with nature is the rule.

EN GEV

This kibbutz situated on the eastern shore of the Sea of Galilee grew was founded in the late 'thirties. Originally this settlement could only be reached by boat from the Sea of Galilee; then because of its location it was a great target for the Syrian forces, until Israel conquered the Golan Heights during the "Six Day War". Today there are excellent connections between En Gev and Tiberias, with regularly scheduled boat service between the two shores. Fishing, but mainly fruit and vegetable farming are the main sources of income. The place is famous throughout the country for its *Music and Folklore Festival* held every Easter. A local restaurant serves "Saint Peter's Fish" (also known as John Dory).

An inviting beach at En Gev.

Hamat Gader seen from above against the Golan Heights.

A panorama of the tourist village at Ramot.

HAMAT GADER

The archeological area of Hamat Gader and the adjacent thermal-recreational area is located southeast of the Sea of Galilee on the banks of the Yarmuk river on the upper piedmont of the Golan heights. The place and its thermal waters have been known since prehistoric times.

Its location, at a point in which the strata of the subsoil are closest to the magma which still "activates" the earth's core, causes the water to heat up as it passes through these layers. On its way to the surface the water is enriched by the natural minerals, salts and radioactivity in the subsoil. The waters gush from four springs at temperatures ranging from 29°C to 51°C. Hydrogen sulfide, radium and radon, are among the various substances found in the waters and render them particularly effective in the treatment of various disorders.

Infrastructures for thermal baths date from ancient times. Traces of baths from the Canaanite period have been discovered, but it was during the Hellenistic era that the area began to prosper continuously up to the present day. During the Hellenistic

period it was known as *Gadara* and was the central point from which Greek culture and civilization were spread through the Holy Land. In those days, animal raising and definitely fishing and sailing on the nearby Sea of Galilee were the most important activities. This assumption is substantiated by archeological findings, especially coins; already the leader of the Galaad territories, it played a primary role among the cities of the Decapolis. Later, this Hellenized area was conquered by Rome and Augustus turned it over to Herod the Great.

Matthew VIII: 28-34 also mentions the place: "...And when he was come to the other side into the country of the Gergesenes, there met him two possessed with devils, coming out of the tombs, exceeding fierce, so that no man might pass by that way.

And, behold, they cried out, saying, What have we to do with thee, Jesus, thou Son of God? art thou come hither to torment us before the time?

And there was a good way of from them an herd of many swine feeding.

So the devils besought him, saying, If thou cast us out, suffer us to go away into the herd of swine.

And he said unto them, Go. And when they were come out, they went into the herd of swine: and, behold, the whole herd of swine ran violently down a steep place into the sea, and perished in the waters.

And they that kept them fled, and went their ways into the city, and told everything, and what was befallen to the possessed of the devils.

And, behold, the whole city came out to meet Jesus: and when they saw him, they besought him that he would depart out of their coasts..."

St. Epiphanus, bishop of Salamis (Cyprus) who lived in the IV century also wrote about the place "...an annual feast brings great multitudes to Gader.

A few charming pictures of the Alligator Park at Hamat Gader and the recreactional facilities. The free-roaming animals, swimming pools, lush vegetation, alligators and the ruins of the ancient Roman baths, make this one of the most attractive and interesting places for tourists and vacationers.

For several days people of all places converge upon the place, anxious to leave their ills in the thermal waters. But even the devil has well laid his traps...since men and women bathe together..."

The excavations of Roman ruins have revealed a Bath Complex which is one of the most incredible examples of this type of architecture in the Middle East and the Roman world in general. It is believed that the Baths at Hamat Gader ranked second in the entire Roman Empire and were extremely popular throughout the II century A.D., and part of the III century, and then were renovated during the VII century. They were abandoned in the IX century and gradually disappeared into the earth as it were. Major excavations, divided into several campaigns,

These pictures of the Roman Baths at Hamat Gadar show some of the architectural details and an excellent view of the "Oval Pool". The well-preserved pool has six marble fountains that filled it with cold water, while the hot water was channeled in from nearby sulphur springs. The bottom picture shows the "Room of the Niches", an open "room" with a pool and 26 marble fountains. Many Byzantine and early Arabian inscriptions have also been found at this site.

starting from the late nineteen seventies have brought to light many well-preserved ruins. Some of the finds include glass bottles, pottery and coins. The ruins of an ancient **theater** also date from Roman times, and the remains of a V century **synagogue** contain a fine mosaic floor and inscriptions in Greek and Aramaic.

Hamat Gader's contemporary reputation, however, is also linked to the modern **Alligator Park** where recreational facilities are provided in inviting settings. The main attraction is a group of alligators from Florida: they live freely in an environment that recreates the atmosphere of a sub-tropical jungle.

A detail of the ancient water pipes from the Roman baths at Hamat Gader.

The so-called "Western Wing", once closed to bathers, housed a sophisticated network of water pipes.

This still-active thermal spring dominates the underlying "Oval Pool".

The Sea of Galilee and lush green crops.

A few interesting pictures of Yardenit and the Jordan River. The site of Jesus' baptism is still visited by many pilgrims.

YARDENIT

BAPTISM OF JESUS - Though not very important from a strictly economic standpoint in ancient times, the river Jordan was of extraordinary religious and symbolic significance.

From the snowy peaks of Mt Hermon, the Jordan runs almost 320 kilometres in twisting loops.

This is the river that marks the boundary of the Promised Land; these are the waters that Moses was not allowed to cross. Joshua crossed them, and the event was solemnly recorded: "Hear, O Israel: Thou art to pass over Jordan this day..." (Deuteronomy, IX 1-3).

On these banks John the Baptist preached, and according to tradition Jesus was baptized there. The "Yardenit" baptismal Centre was built by members of the nearby Kinneret kibbutz to receive the great numbers of pilgrims that go to the place; in these waters the Greek Orthodox and Catholic faithful symbolically renew their baptism. "Then cometh Jesus from Galilee to Jordan unto John, to be baptized of him. But John forbad him, saying, I have need to be baptized of thee, and comest thou to me? And Jesus answering said unto him, Suffer it to be so now: for thus it becometh us to fulfil all righteousness. Then he suffered him" (Matthew, III 13-15).

The impressive ruins of the immense crusader fortress at Belvoir.

BELVOIR

The important ruins of this ancient fortress stand out on top of a steep hill to the right of the Jordan River. Being the highest point near where the Jordan and Yarmuk rivers converge it offers an excellent view of the surrounding area: from the valley below to distant territories, rewarding those who have made the climb either on foot or horseback as in ancient times.

This impressive fortified complex dates from XII century. It was long a key part of the crusaders' defences in the Holy Land.

Subsequently purchased by the Order of the Hospital of St. John of Jerusalem (precursor of the Knights of Malta which exist even today) and re-

These pictures reveal the current condition of the ruins of the crusader fortress at Belvoir: portions of wall made of squared porphyry blocks, parts of the interior and a detail of the inner courtyard.

mained in crusader hands until it was captured by Saladin after a drawn-out siege. In the past it has been known as *Kochav Ha' Yarden* (Star of the Jordan) in Hebrew, while the Arabs called it *Kaukab el-Harva* (Star of the Winds). The place had yet another name, *Agrippina*, a stronghold of the Zealots the group of Jewish extremists who bitterly fought the Roman troops that occupied the Holy Land in the first century. The fortress, or rather what remains of it, is one of the most fascinating attractions in the National Park.

Of the ancient rectangular foundations, we can see the remains of the colossal scarp walls that were built with huge blocks of squared stone. Some Jewish symbols have been found carved into the crusader walls. Originally the fortress was defended by a deep moat on three sides. Excavations in the mid-seventies have revealed ancient homes nearby.

Here we see some details of the large Roman Theater at Bet She'an. Part of the outer perimeter, the cavea and the stage with excavations going on can be seen.

BET SHE'AN

Modern Bet She'an is a new city located in the part of the Jordan Valley from which it gets its name. To the west it faces the Valley of Jezreel while on the east we have the roads leading to Syria (the famous "cease fire line" is just a short distance away along the banks of the Jordan) Its fortunate geographic setting and exceptionally fertile ground contributed to its being an ideal link between North and South, East and West through its centuries of history. From Syria to Egypt and from the banks of the Jordan to the shores of the Mediterranean, Bet She'an has been an essential crossroad on the area's most important thoroughfares.

The first settlements in the area date from the fourth millenium B.C. This hypothesis is supported by the archeologists who, in the nineteentwenties and thirties, uncovered 18 layers: including traces of Egyptian control between the XV and XII centuries B.C. Its great variety of agricultural products, made possible thanks to abundant natural water resources, led to its being dubbed "Gate of Paradise". During the Greek period it was known as *Scythopolis*. The Jewish settlers were wiped out during the Jewish Wars, the settlements reflourished and prospered even under Arab dominion, and at least up to the Crusades when the territory began a steady decline.

Among the archeological treasures at Bet She'an, the *Roman Theater* is worthy of special mention. It is the largest structure of its kind in Israel and dates from around the III century A.D. when it was capable of hosting audiences of up to 8,000. Both the cavea and the stage are excellently preserved. And all around we can see the excavations of many Roman streets and other period buildings.

An interesting glimpse of the vast archeological area at Bet She'an. Although the Roman Theater is the most significant part, the other buildings certainly should not be overlooked: sections of Roman roads, walls, fragments of columns and other vestiges are scattered about this fascinating natural scenario of the Galilee.

The synagogue at Katzrin and an interior view.

Two pictures of the archeological area at Tel Hazor
and the excavations.

KATZRIN

The main Israeli administrative center, in this "hot" frontier area, at the foot of the Golan Heights, in the upper part of the Jordan Valley, Katzrin offers the visitor an interesting view of the ruins of an ancient Jewish settlemen that prospered during Roman and Byzantine times. The remains of the **synagogue** and other public buildings are particularly interesting; in the past the ancient ruins were used as a source of stone to build a nearby Arab village.

TEL HAZOR

The ruins of Tel Hazor are located on the opposite side of the valley, facing Katzrin. This biblical Canaanite city, has at least 3,000 years of history and was razed to the ground at least 20 times over the millenia. Destruction and rebuilding on the same site have created an artificial hill ("tel"). Excavations, undertaken in 1928 and in the mid-fifties, have brought to light traces of the many overlapping settlements, an aqueduct and a basalt *lion*, symbol of the ancient city.

KIBBUTZ AYELET HASHAHAR

In 1918 Kibbutz Ayelet Hashahar was founded near the archeological site of Tel Hazor. The kibbutz maintains a museum in which are housed fascinating artifact gathered from Tel Hazor, the most powerful city in the area at the time of Joshua's entry into Canaan. Vases, jewelery, spearheads and basalt statuettes were found during excavation of the site which began in 1928. The digs brought to light a lower city and an acropolis connected by a tunnel 38 meters deep, numerous princely tombs, a palace, a great temple with numerous cult objects and the tomb of the king of Hazor named in the Book of Joshua (XI, 10) and in the Book of Judges (IV, 2).

Tel Hazor, a detail of the archeological area.

Various views of the Kibbutz Ayelet Hashahar, whose name means "morning star".

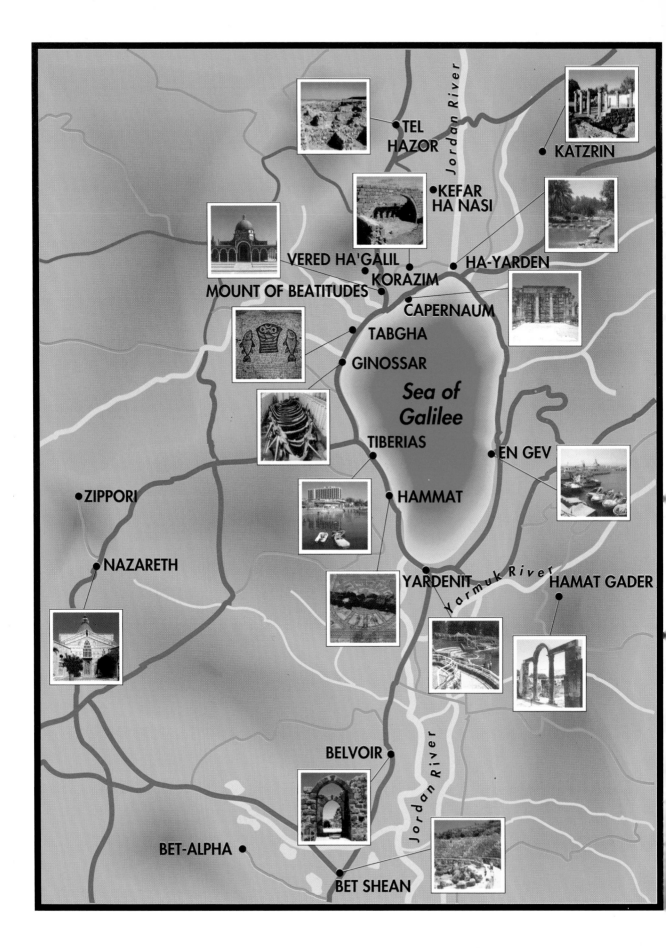

TEL HAZOR

KATZRIN

KEFAR HA NASI

VERED HA'GALIL

HA-YARDEN

KORAZIM

MOUNT OF BEATITUDES

CAPERNAUM

TABGHA

GINOSSAR

Sea of Galilee

TIBERIAS

EN GEV

ZIPPORI

HAMMAT

NAZARETH

YARDENIT

Yarmuk River

HAMAT GADER

Jordan River

BELVOIR

Jordan River

BET-ALPHA

BET SHEAN